bush
PUBLISHING
& associates

AMAZING PARENTING

BECOMING AN AMAZING PARENT AND HAVING AMAZING CHILDREN THROUGH GRACE-BASED PARENTING

SAMUEL MARTINEZ

COPYRIGHT

AMAZING PARENTING-Becoming an Amazing Parent and Having Amazing Children Through Grace-Based Parenting

ISBN: 978-1-7329751-2-5
Copyright © 2019 Pastor Samuel Martinez

Bush Publishing & Associates, LLC., books may be ordered everywhere and Amazon.com

For further information, please contact:
Bush Publishing & Associates www.bushpublishing.com

Printed in the United States of America.

DEDICATION

To all parents who desire to do the right things with their children yet find themselves struggling with not knowing what to do, resulting in guilt, shame, fear, and condemnation. I have been there. God is on your side. He can help.

And to all who have instructed me on parenting, including David, Solomon, the Apostle Paul, my mother Angela, my wife, my Pastors and Teachers and last but not least, my son Andrés, great nephews and great niece- Andrew, Oscar and Giselle.

Special thanks to Helen McLeod, who tirelessly read and reread this manuscript.

For while the Law was given through Moses,
Grace (*unearned, undeserved favor* and spiritual blessings) and
truth came through Jesus Christ.
(italics mine) John 1:17, Amplified Bible

And since it is through God's kindness, then it
is not by their good works. For in that case,
God's grace would not be what it really is-*free
and undeserved.* (italics mine)
Romans 11:6, New Living Translation

GRACE -

GOD'S

UNEARNED

UNDERSERVED

UNMERITED FAVOR

TABLE OF CONTENTS

INTRODUCTION

Society has changed drastically over the last several decades. There are many reasons for this, but a major one is that we have moved away from the biblical model of grace-based parenting. I will not reminisce about the "good old days of parenting," because even my parents' generation did not totally follow the Biblical model of parenting. However, parenting was still easier back in the days of our parents and grandparents. Society has changed. TV, the internet, cell phones, and social media have brought monumental changes into our lives. And yet, the needs of our children and youth have remained the same.

The changes in our society have just made it more important than ever to rely on the Bible for help and direction. The Bible is not outdated, and grace-based parenting is needed more than ever. But why grace-based parenting? Because we are now in the new covenant which is the covenant of grace. Furthermore, grace is the gospel. The gospel of grace needs to be the basis of our parenting.

In Galatians 1:6-7, Paul stated that the Galatians had departed themselves from Him that had called them in the grace of Christ into another gospel that he stated was not another gospel. They had departed from the gospel (good news) of the grace of Christ. Therefore, grace is the gospel.

The gospel is the good news of the grace of Christ. Note that in Acts 20:24 Paul stated the same thing. Furthermore, in Romans 1:16 Paul stated that the gospel is the power of God unto salvation. Hence, as we bring the gospel (grace) into our homes, we bring the power of God into our parenting. It is that simple.

Grace speaks to us of a God that loves us unconditionally and eternally. It speaks to us of the forgiveness of our sins and that God is not holding our sins against us since Jesus has come and paid for all our sins (2 Corinthians 5:19). On top of this, He has declared us His very righteousness, a righteousness that Daniel called an everlasting righteousness (Daniel 9:24).

John 1:17 (Amplified Version, AMPC) states that grace is the unearned, undeserved favor of God. Get a revelation of this, parents, that the unearned and undeserved favor of God is available to you in your parenting (and every area in life for that matter), even when you do not do everything exactly right. The old covenant of the law demanded that we keep all the commandments to be blessed. Under the covenant of grace, we are already blessed (Ephesians 1:3, Galatians 3:13-14).

Grace calls us to receive by faith the finished work of Jesus. As already noted, Romans 1:16 states that the gospel is the power of God unto salvation. We have limited the definition of the word salvation to deliverance from hell, but in the Greek, the definition includes health, safety, rescue, preservation, and prosperity. In essence, His power to live the abundant life that Jesus came to bring us. Of course, this includes amazing parenting. To reiterate, if we bring grace (which is the gospel) into our parenting, we bring the power of God into it. We can then have success in our parenting far beyond our natural abilities and skills. This is the favor of God. You can see that grace and favor can be used interchangeably.

Parents, God is for you. He knows parenting can be tough. Look at the problems HE has with His children. Yet, He still loves us. He is our model. Do not give up on yourself or your children. Before Jesus returns, we will see millions of our children coming back to the Father of mercies and the God of all comfort. God is truly turning the hearts of the parents to their children (Luke 1:17). The book of Malachi adds that God will also turn the hearts of the children to their parents. However, it starts with the hearts of the parents turned to their children. Note also that Luke 1:17 eliminates the curse noted in Malachi 4 since Jesus took the curse. Our generation is about to see an outpouring upon our children like never before.

As you read and learn to apply grace to your parenting, a key to remember is that we cannot change our children. We are not even responsible for changing them. God is. He will change them as we simply stay with the guidance of the

Holy Spirit and put our trust in God. I am not denying the free will of your children. I am simply calling all parents to rest. Grace calls us to rest trusting Him that He is working. We do create an environment for change, then leave the results to Him.

Be blessed as you read. Read this book slowly. I prefer parents read only one or two chapters per day. If you do read it all in one sitting, go over the book again slowly. Some truths are repeated for emphasis.

One great thought before going on in the book. Amazing parenting is birthed in amazing marriages. I did not state perfect marriages. I do not address this in detail in this book, but parents need to work on their marriages along with their parenting. For this reason, the Lord had me finish *Amazing Marriage* at the same time I finished this book on parenting. I pray that God enlightens your eyes to His great love for you and the capacity that He has given you to be an amazing parent!

CHAPTER ONE

ACCEPT GOD'S FORGIVENESS

Parents, this is where we have to start. If you cannot accept God's forgiveness, it will be a challenge to hear from the Lord instructions concerning your parenting. Furthermore, without accepting God's forgiveness, your parenting will not be grace-based parenting but guilt-based parenting. Therefore, whatever you have done right, thank the Lord. Whatever you have not done just right, remember that there is no condemnation to those in Christ Jesus (Romans 8:1, NLT). Our sins and lawless deeds He remembers no more (Hebrews 8:12). Condemnation kills. Paul called the law (the old covenant) the ministry of death in 2 Corinthians chapter 3. However, Jesus brought us grace and did not come to condemn us (John 3:17).

You cannot begin a life of grace-based parenting without first receiving His forgiveness into your life. 2 Corinthians 5:19 clearly states that God is not holding our sins against us. Why? Because Jesus paid for all of them. In Romans 4:8, King David speaks of the blessedness of the man to whom the Lord will not impute sin. Before you continue with this book, take time to read Ephesians 1:7, Colossians 1:14, 1 John 2:12 and Colossians 2:13.

If Jesus is your Lord and Savior, then receive by faith that you are (present tense) forgiven of all your past, present and future sins. When Jesus died all our sins were future so accept that even your future sins are forgiven. Reject the thought that because of past wrong decisions in your parenting God is punishing you. Jesus took our punishment. Actually, knowing all your sins are forgiven helps you be honest with God when you do miss it.

Remember the woman in John chapter 8? You probably know that Jesus told the woman, "Neither do I condemn you. Go and sin no more." For years, I had problems with this verse since I cannot tell even the godliest person in my church to "sin no more." Years later, I learned that Jesus gave her a gift. It was the gift of no condemnation, and if she received it, she would no longer go around jumping into the arms of another man who was not her husband. Grace would change her and empower her by filling her with the love that no man could give her. When she received the gift, she no longer thought of herself as an adulterous woman, but a forgiven one. I like to say it this way. Jesus did not tell her not to sin again. He empowered her not to. I do not believe that she ever fell again into the arms of a man who was not her husband. Therefore, in that sense, she "sinned no more."

Accept God's forgiveness even when you miss it. You can then hear what God is writing on your mind and heart (Hebrews 8:10-12). Of course, we accept responsibility and repent (as we want our children to do as well) when we miss it, but condemnation is to be rejected. Repentance is a change of thinking that leads to a change in behavior. Change your thinking now to this truth. You are forgiven. God is for you.

Why not pray this simple prayer before we move on?

Dear Father, thank You that because of the cross of Jesus and His shed blood I am forgiven of all my sins past, present and future. My sins and lawless deeds You remember no more. I reject all condemnation, guilt, and shame, and receive the gift of no condemnation, in Jesus' name, Amen.

Now, reject the thought that when a person learns they are totally forgiven, they will sin more. Jesus did not think so when He stated that the person who is forgiven little (no one really since we have all been forgiven much) only loves little (Luke 7:47 NLT). Turn this around, and we see that the person who then <u>recognizes</u> that they have been forgiven much loves much. Look up; you have taken a big first step in becoming an amazing parent!

CHAPTER TWO

RECEIVE HIS GRACE

John 1:17 states that the law was given through Moses, but grace (His unearned, undeserved favor) came through Jesus our Lord (see AMPC version). The old covenant has been done away with, and the new has come (Hebrews 8:8-13). As a Christian and as a parent, you need divine help. The Christian life is impossible to live in our own efforts. That is what the Old Testament saints felt that they could do when it came to the law. They failed miserably. Grace supplies what in the natural we do not have to live a successful Christian life and be amazing parents.

Listen, parents, God does not want us living any aspect of our lives without Him. This is what is to distinguish us from the world. We wake up in the morning and quickly receive His grace. Our success as parents will either be from our self-effort or His grace (favor). I think I will take His favor. It made Joseph a success, and it will make you one too. Grace does not lead to inactivity. It leads to Holy Spirit inspired actions.

Have you noticed that the Apostle Paul always began his epistles by declaring grace over the recipients of his letters?

He did this because he wanted them to stop at the beginning of His letters and receive God's grace (His favor). This needs to be an action of ours not just in the beginning of the day, but every time we are faced with a task to complete. It is good to stop and say, "Father, today I receive your grace. I do not want to rely on my ability and education. I lean on your unearned and undeserved favor." Receive His grace even or especially when you miss it. Think about this. Our Heavenly Father wants to do us favors every day.

Jesus did not state, "Come unto me all you who labor and are heavy laden and I will give you more rules and laws." No, He gives more grace. John 1:16 (AMPC Version) shows us that one grace after another is available to us. Someone likened it to one wave after another. The problem is that we do not feel we deserve it, and you are right. That is why it is called grace–God's unearned favor. We could not and cannot do anything to deserve it. It is a gift to be received. In fact, Paul stated in Romans 5:17 that <u>abundance</u> of grace is available to us if we will just receive it. The word "receive" in this verse is in present active tense. We are to be receiving an abundance of God's favor continually.

God is on our side. He is not against us. Receive His grace and be empowered to become what in the natural you have struggled to become - an amazing parent!

CHAPTER THREE

ULTIMATE GOAL OF PARENTING – TEACHING OUR CHILDREN GOD'S LOVE, PART ONE

The ultimate goal of parenting is to communicate and build into our children that God loves them totally, unconditionally, with no strings attached. This means that as soon as they are born, in deed and in word, we communicate <u>our</u> love for them. As they grow older, we begin teaching them, from the Bible, how much God loves them. Teach them that Jesus loved them so much He died for them. If they are younger, read them Bible stories about characters, such as David, and apply the love of God to the stories. For example, David means beloved. David beat Goliath because he knew God loved him. As our children learn God loves them, they will take down the giants in their lives.

The stories of Jesus are especially good to read to our children when they are younger, but even our teens need to get a revelation of the compassion of our Savior who went about doing good and healing all (Acts 10:38). The end result of teaching our children about the love of God is for them to see Jesus as their friend and constant companion. Knowing <u>about</u> Jesus and His teaching can make our children religious. Knowing Jesus is life transforming (2 Corinthians 3:18).

We cannot communicate the great, unconditional love of God to our children without a revelation of our Abba Father's love for us (Romans 8:15). Parents let's face it. We parent the way we were parented, and our children will parent the way they are parented. The concept we have of our Heavenly Father, the inner image we have of Him, will be communicated unconsciously to our children. The concept we have of God will color ALL our parenting.

To get a revelation of God's love, read scriptures on the love of God daily. There are many good books on the love of God. My book *Amazing Love* is a simple way to start learning about God's love. Make it a lifetime endeavor to learn more and more about God's love. Thank Him every day for loving you even when you may not feel His love for you. In thanking Him, you receive. If you have hurts from your past, receiving His love will heal them. Don't you think the woman in John chapter 8 (mentioned in chapter one) was full of hurts? I am convinced that as she received God's grace and love and the gift of no condemnation she was healed. Receiving the love and grace of God also releases us to forgive. Forgiven people forgive. Loved people (those with a revelation of God's love for them) love.

Now let's return to teaching our children that they are loved. As they grow older, drugs, gangs, and promiscuity will have little to no allure. When they leave home with a revelation of (and not just a mental understanding of) God's love, they will pass it on to their children. Therefore, tell them every day that you love them, and that God loves them. Tell them He has great plans for their lives even when they misbehave. Let them know that you are well pleased with them as God communicated to His Own Son our Savior in Matthew 3:17.

Of course, you do not always like what they do, but they are still well pleasing to you. We love them when they do well, and we love them when they frustrate us. We never want them to believe that our love is based on their performance, as God does not want us to believe that His love for us is based on our performance. Someone said that God loves us even in our worse day. And we will do the same with our children. Our demonstrations of love toward our children open their hearts to us, but more importantly, to receive that Jesus loves them.

Folks, <u>this</u> is grace, and grace empowers heart change and victory over temptation (Romans 6:14). The goodness of God leads people to repentance (Romans 2:4). Returning to Matthew 3:17, up to that point the Bible does not mention any miracle or other similar act that Jesus had done for the Father. Immediately after hearing the words from His

Father, He faced temptation and overcame it. Our children also will overcome temptation as they recognize the love and grace of God (Romans 8:37). Furthermore, as soon as Jesus heard those words from His Father, He started His ministry. In a similar way, our children will be equipped to fulfill the call of God on their lives as they hear and receive that they are beloved. May all our children leave home with the reality in their hearts that they are beloved.

Do we discipline them when they violate a rule? Of course, we do. However, after any discipline, we remind them of our love for them. Love and grace must be the last thing they hear from us after we discipline them. Actually, love and grace should be the first and last thing they hear from us. And finally, parents, initiate love. Particularly with our teens, we cannot wait for them to show us love.

As you read the next few chapters, you will learn more from a practical point how to teach them the love of God. Of course, it bears mentioning not just to tell them, but demonstrate it. This is a key when parenting teenagers. Teens are behaviorally oriented, which means they want love demonstrated. In other words, we tell them we love them, and then in actions we show them our love and God's love. Don't quit now. You are just getting started. You are becoming an amazing parent!

CHAPTER FOUR

———◆•✦•◆———

ULTIMATE GOAL OF PARENTING, PART TWO

G od's love is eternal. It has no beginning and has no end. It is unconditional. If we grew up with parents that only loved us when we did everything right, came down on us hard with every little thing we did wrong, or expected perfection from us, then we will have a wrong image of God. God is no longer angry with us even when we sin (Isaiah 54:9). His love is what brings us to heart repentance (Romans 2:4), and heart change (and not just behavioral modification) is what God wants from us, and we want from our children.

But isn't God a God of justice too? Yes, but God's justice was completely satisfied when Jesus paid for all our sins. He is not holding our sins against us (2 Corinthians 5:19). Of course, we discipline our children but never say anything like "God is going to get you for that" or that God is angry with them. When our children sin (and they will; parents, we sin too), we want them to run to us, but ultimately **to** God, and not **from** Him.

There is nothing we can do to cause God to love us more or to love us less. This brings great security to our lives and our children. Now, in case you have heard that by teaching grace, people will think they have a license to sin, no real Christian is looking for a license to sin. However, I have discovered that far too many Christians are looking for a way out of the big three - guilt, condemnation, and shame. The key, parents, is not to use these three to try to bring change in our children. Have more faith in grace, which is Jesus (John 1:17). Grace is not a Bible topic. Grace is a person, our Savior Himself.

Do we really want our children to think that God only loves them when they do everything right? In a similar fashion, we do not want our children to think that we only love them when they do everything right or when they do something outstanding. I will say it again. A revelation of God's love causes children to grow up securely. They will grow up with a victory over fear. 1 John 4:18 shows that perfect love casts out fear. Perfect love is not our love for Him, but a revelation of His love for us. Helping our children live fear free is a major task of parenting and could be a chapter in and of itself. However, I have put this task under this chapter because a revelation of God's love is the number one way to help our children overcome and grow without fear.

We live in such a terror-filled world that stresses out parents as to how to talk to their children about terrorists, violence in schools, and killings in our neighborhoods. When violence appears inexplicable to us as adults, imagine how our children feel. Thank God for the Holy Spirit in us to teach us how to talk with our children. Relax, parents. We may not always say everything correctly to our children, but when they know your love and God's love, things work out. It is our presence they need more than anything else, and a constant reminder of God's love and our love. I will talk more later about how to train our children to live protected in a violent world. Hey, God loves you. You are becoming an amazing parent!

CHAPTER FIVE

---◆◆◆◆◆◆◆---

THE IMPORTANCE OF WORDS

I will never forget hearing as a young Christian many years ago that children are word-made. The Bible is full of references to the importance of words. Proverbs 18:21 states that death and life are in the power of the tongue.

So, parents never use words that label or put down your children. I know that many times in our desperation to get our children to change we label them as stupid, dumb, disobedient or rebellious. This is not helpful, but hurtful. In correcting our children, do what our Heavenly Father does. Deal with their behavior, but do not attack their value as a person. Yes, I know that at times God called His people rebellious and disobedient in the Old Testament, but remember we are now in the dispensation of grace.

In my parenting classes, I address what I call Shaming Statements. I will address this area more fully later. Suffice it to state for now that statements that put a person down are damaging. The previous chapter mentioned the big three that many parents use to try to get their children to obey--condemnation, guilt, and shame. All three are expressed through words.

If we define grace as God's unearned and undeserved favor, then in Ephesians 4:29 Paul is telling us never to speak words that do not communicate God's unearned and undeserved favor. This does not mean we never correct, but Colossians 4:6 states that our speech should always be with grace. Correct with grace. Grace deals with the actions of our children but does not attack their sense of value.

OK, so we see the importance of <u>avoiding</u> hurtful words. However, it is as hurtful when no uplifting, loving words are <u>shared.</u> Silence is not golden here. I have often stated that no child should ever go to bed without at least one meaningful touch and something loving having been said by mom and dad. Lately, I have begun to see the need for several touches and loving words shared with our children due to the increase in bullying at school. Concerned about your child being bullied? Don't be. Speak the blood of Jesus over them, the protection of the angels, and keep filling your children with words of love, grace, and praise. You can see the appendix for some examples, but all parents know our children at the least need to hear "good morning," "goodnight," and "I love you." Girls need to hear how lovely and precious they are, and both sexes need to hear how pleased we are with their accomplishments, even if (should I say especially when) in the eyes of others it was just a minor accomplishment. And if they go out for something like a sport or a part in a play and fail, let them hear that for you they are still your champions.

In praising our children, we need to use expressive words. For example, if a child draws a picture for a parent, saying "Thank you" is fine. Being expressive is saying things such as, "Wow, for me?" Or even, "Look at these colors," and "You were so thoughtful." If a child tries over and over to succeed in a task and finally does it, say, "You really persevered, sweetheart, way to go." You just praised your child and taught her a new word. You are amazing!

As I stated previously, even Jesus needed to hear words of love and encouragement from His Father. In the Mount of Transfiguration (Matthew chapter 17), Jesus heard, "This is My beloved Son, in whom I am well pleased. Hear Him!" Later, in 2 Peter 1:17, Peter remarked that Jesus received honor and glory when these words came to Him. Likewise, our children will receive honor and glory when they hear words of grace from our lips. Stop and let this sink in.

Another area related to the importance of words in the lives of our children occurs when they are persecuted for their faith. Our words not only help them when they are made fun of for their faith but reminds them that Jesus mentioned in Matthew 5:11-12 to rejoice and be glad when mistreated for their love for the Lord. Actually, our children receive honor and glory from the Lord when they stand up for Him and are persecuted. They need to know this. Teach them to dare to be different. Dare to be a Daniel. As God's masterpiece (Ephesians 2:10, NLT), they ARE different and unique.

We have heard that one word from God can change a life forever. Likewise, a word from a parent can do the same. Solomon spoke of a "word fitly spoken" in Proverbs 25:11 and added that it is "wonderful to say the right thing at the right time" in Proverbs 15:23 (NLT). The person who said something about sticks and stones hurting but not words was terribly wrong. Hurtful words hurt more than physical objects. Not everyone will like our children as they are growing up. They will be rejected sooner or later by someone. No need to worry parents. You are setting them up to overcome when you feed them grace-filled words every day. Look up; you are becoming an amazing parent!

CHAPTER SIX

+-⚙️◈⚙️-+

THE IMPORTANCE OF TOUCH

Children cannot live or thrive without touch. The Bible is full of examples. In Matthew, the 8th chapter, a man with leprosy came running to Jesus questioning if it was Jesus' will to heal him. Jesus told the man that it was His will to heal him, but, first of all, He touched him. As a man with leprosy, no one would touch him. This man undoubtedly yearned for a touch from someone.

In another biblical account, mothers brought their children to Jesus to touch them. Mothers know how important touch is. When the disciples brushed the mothers and children aside, Jesus rebuked them.

Let me take you to Bogota Colombia in the late '70s. Premature babies were dying at an alarming rate. Several doctors began placing premature babies in the mothers' blouses as soon as they were born. When they needed a break, the fathers would carry them under their shirts. The mortality rate went down drastically. This method goes today by several names such as Kangaroo Care or Kangaroo Mother Care.

Touch communicates value and draws people together. Lack of it draws people apart and causes children to question their value to their parents. As they grow older children, may not always want to be kissed or hugged. When your teenager is sitting at the dinner table, come from behind and just tap him on the shoulder gently. Look for the opportunities.

Children need the touch of both parents. I remember over 25 years ago when I did my first class on parenting, being impressed by the Lord to tell parents that the first thing all children need is two parents actively involved in their lives. I will share tips to single parents later. Men need to hug their children, or at least give them several meaningful touches every day. Furthermore, fathers, when your girls start developing physically and emotionally, do not draw back. This really applies to both sexes, but even more for our girls. We want our girls (as they grow older) to look for a guy that treats them like dad did. We do not want them looking for father's love in guys only looking out for themselves. It has been said that a picture is worth a thousand words. I would say a touch is worth ten thousand words. How about a touch along with a grace-filled word? Priceless! Enough said. You are becoming an amazing parent!

CHAPTER SEVEN

FORGIVE

As parents, we forgive our children when they do wrong, not when they ASK for forgiveness. Now if we are honest with ourselves, we can admit that at times we wait until they come and ask for forgiveness before we forgive them. However, what pattern did our Heavenly Father give us? In Chapter One we saw that we are forgiven, present tense. Since we have received Jesus as our Lord and Savior, all our sins are forgiven. When we do sin, we can be honest and open with God and run to Him and not from Him because we have already been forgiven.

Remember the prodigal son? Did his dad forgive him when he asked for forgiveness? Dad hugged him before the little speech which he had rehearsed. I do not believe the son had really repented before his father showed him grace. He was just hungry, and by becoming a servant, he thought he could fill his hunger.

Our forgiveness is grace and grace provides the environment that will move our children to come and ask for forgiveness. This forgiveness is for their benefit, not so they will recognize that mom and dad were right to begin with. Do not think that I am saying just to excuse (or not discipline) their behavior. We will discuss correction more in the next chapter. Just to let it go is frankly poor parenting. It takes more effort and work to discipline. To forgive before they ask for forgiveness will assure that our discipline will be out of love and not out of wanting to get even. Furthermore, as we forgive, we go free.

We are not just to forgive the major events, but forgive the rolling of the eyes, their attitudes, and even their thoughtlessness. Again, I am not saying not to address their behavior. The issue is that many times (I am sure you have discovered this by now, parents) our children push our buttons. Unless we consistently forgive, resentments will build up. Lean on the grace of God and remind yourselves that you can forgive with the help of our Father because we have been forgiven. Forgive as an act of your will and in obedience to the Word whether you feel like it or not.

But what if I forgive and discipline, but my child still does not come to ask for forgiveness? What if I do not see any repentance? Well, we are actually talking about two different things here, forgiveness and repentance. If we forgive and even if they ask for forgiveness and we do not notice any change in their mindset or thinking (repentance), then (as an example) I may still not let my teenager use my car or go out past a certain time. The issue, parents, is that I can forgive, but if I see no change in their thinking patterns about the issue at hand, then we do not necessarily have to trust them.

Repentance is not just saying that they are sorry. Repentance, biblically, is a change in thinking (Romans 12:2), which leads to a change in behavior. The Greek word for repentance, metanoia, means a change in one's mind. Our children can say they are sorry and change their outward behavior without changing their way of believing and thinking, without truly repenting. Ultimately, this book is all about helping our children not just change their outward behavior. We are after inner transformation, as stated in Romans 12:2 and 2 Corinthians 3:18. That is what God desires from us and our children.

How can we know if our children have repented, changed their way of believing and thinking, and not just saying they are sorry to get the car back? Well, this is why we talk to them and trust the Holy Spirit to help us. More on this in chapter 19. But the key in this chapter is that forgiveness does not mean I do not discipline or immediately trust them again. It just means I let go of resentments.

Let's go back to what to do if we forgive our children and they still do not ask for forgiveness. Well, there are a few important things we can do. First of all, check your heart to make sure you <u>have</u> forgiven. Secondly, continue to love them. Thirdly, use your faith. Romans 2:4 states that the goodness of God leads to repentance. As you have forgiven, the goodness of God has been released. Stay in faith. Keep the switch of faith turned on. Keep believing that the goodness of God **is** leading your child to repentance. Do not give up. Put patience (consistency) to work. You are becoming an amazing parent!

CHAPTER EIGHT

GRACE-BASED CORRECTION

Correction should deal with what they did (the DO) but is not to damage their sense of value (the WHO). In other words, no words that attack them, but words that deal with their behavior. Even calling our children disobedient is not in line with the word of God. Yes, they disobeyed, but be careful with <u>labeling</u> your child as disobedient. I can remind them that they disobeyed without labeling them disobedient children.

Again, parents, it is extremely important that we avoid the use of condemnation, guilt, and shame in an attempt to get our children to change. When parents are exasperated and have tried all they know, they use these as the nuclear option. Other parents use these three exclusively in parenting. Though these three may bring some outward change, they do not change the heart. Actually, they damage it.

When Paul brought correction, he reminded the people of who they were in Christ. He reminded them clearly that they were the temple of the Holy Spirit on one occasion (1 Corinthians 3:16, 2 Corinthians 6:16), and told them to awake to righteousness and sin not in another occasion (1 Corinthians 15:34). When the Lord corrected the churches in the second and third chapters of Revelation, Jesus looked for what He could say good about them, corrected them and then gave them a final word of encouragement. Let the last words that a child hears after you discipline them be how much you love them and how much they are loved by God.

Folks, this takes practice, but we have the Holy Spirit to remind us and the grace of our Lord that empowers us. Speak to the Spirit of God to remind you to discipline in grace and receive the grace of God every day. Furthermore, as you rely on the Holy Spirit (more on this later), He will show you what will be an appropriate discipline for the particular area of disobedience. However, discipline is not just about correcting bad behavior, but also about encouraging good habits such as cleaning their room, eating healthy food, and learning good manners.

Ultimately, in grace-based parenting, the emphasis is more on encouraging good behavior than correcting bad behavior. Hence, anytime a child does something right, acknowledge it. Someone stated that it is easier to encourage good behavior than to stop bad behavior. Think about this. When a child does something we do not like, we quickly tell them about it. Sadly, we tend to let good behavior go unacknowledged. Ah, but we are learning.

Grace gives us (and our children) the power to overcome sin according to Romans 6:14. Hence, as we correct in grace, we empower them to overcome bad behavior and the temptations of the devil. The world's way of NOT disciplining because they do not want to hurt their self-esteem actually hurts their identity. Grace truly reminds them of their true identity as children of the Most High who loves them dearly.

But what if you have a child out of control deliberately breaking curfew, using drugs or alcohol, or other similar behavior? First of all, do not be afraid to get help. Start with the resources in your church. With children out of control, the setting of boundaries and clear expectations are even more important. If rules are broken, consequences need to be given swiftly and firmly every time. However, do not throw out the other 30 chapters in this book. Be consistent. If you have sought God for wisdom and direction, do not bend the rules, but always keep one hand on grace. No, keep both hands on grace.

Keeping both hands on grace reminds us that we need to be aware of the "why" of our children's misbehavior. A young child may simply be tired. An older child may be crying out for attention. Even a child who feels overly protected may have problems expressing this and simply misbehaves. In essence, a child with a love tank (more on this imaginary tank later) will misbehave quicker than a child feeling loved. Thank God for the Holy Spirit who can reveal these things to us. More on the Holy Spirit and His help later as well. The key is when getting ready to discipline to be aware of these factors.

An intervention that I recommend parents use with a child out-of-control or getting there is a family meeting with dad and mom. In this meeting, both parents need to share how they are feeling. I know parents feel overwhelmed with the constant breaking of the rules and constantly having to give consequences to an out-of-control child or youth. I am sure the child or youth is probably overwhelmed as well with the constant harping on them and what they see as the incessant fault finding.

Sit down in the living room and share your feelings. No criticism, no fault-finding, no reminding them of the rules they are breaking (they have heard enough of that I am sure), only the sharing of your fears, that you are feeling overwhelmed and are afraid you are losing them. If there are other things you are feeling, share them as well. But do not attack, and don't forget to share your love for them.

If the child shares something in this type of meeting that is good. However, if they stay silent once you share your feelings, tell the child thank you for listening. The change in your son or daughter may not happen overnight, but it can start overnight.

Grace mandates the rules be clear and specific. To tell a child when dropped off at school "to be good" is unclear. To tell an adolescent to try harder in a particular class is unclear as well. State what specific expectations you have. Furthermore, all children should know and understand the specific consequences for the violation of a rule. For example, before taking them out to a store or their favorite fast food establishment, remind them of the rules. If they break the rules, there should be consequences, like not taking them with you the next time or coming home immediately from the fast food restaurant.

Many times, when working with parents who have children with problematic behavior, I ask what they have already done to correct it. I usually discover that they have threatened, yelled, and pleaded. With no consequences, negative behavior continues. I should add, however, that the consequence should fit the rule violation. Do not be like the parent who grounded for a month when a day would have sufficed. When a serious issue occurs (such as alcohol use), a 72-hour grounding may be needed, but let the Holy Spirit guide you. Grounding to me means being restricted to their rooms with no privileges except to read.

Hence, do not take this chapter to mean firmness with our children is not grace. In fact, I have often stated in my parenting classes that parents should avoid using the word "please" when giving orders. For example, avoid, "Please stop fighting with your sister." "Please pass the butter" is acceptable and models good manners. Many times, frustrated parents yell such things as, "please quiet down" or "please do what I say!" In these examples, the parent is pleading, and pleading decreases their respect for us. In the same manner, yelling lessens their respect for us. Remember the proverb: He who yells loses, but he that stays calm lives to fight another day. Just kidding. Well, maybe I am not.

Ultimately, parents, the greatest discipline is to remind them of their identity in Christ. Remind them of it. Do not preach it to them. I am assuming that you have already led your child to the Lord since most children can receive Jesus by around 5 or 6. If your child has not received Jesus, then remind them of your love for them. However, if they have received the Lord, remind them that they are children of the living God, that they are loved, forgiven, and the righteousness of God in Christ. We remind them of these things at their age level. Rest, parents, more thoughts on grace-based correction will be given in numerous chapters to follow. You are becoming amazing parents!

CHAPTER NINE

LESS IS BEST, MORE GRACE-BASED CORRECTION

Parents, we need to realize that when we are too wordy, our children tune us out. When I have had parents in my office, I time the responses that I recommend that they need to give their children in typical parent/child conflicts. Less is best means get to the point and do not belabor the issue. Most of the times when we have to correct them, the correction can be done in 60 seconds or so. Some things can even be stated in one word such as "No." I will talk more later about saying no to our children and not being afraid to say no, but here I am talking about avoiding lengthy lectures and sermons.

I am not talking about having conversations with your children about sex, life decisions, or the like. But even then, long lectures are not needed unless they are asking questions. Our children can detect when we are talking to them out of genuine concern or when we are talking down to them.

Maybe I need to give an example. If your son or daughter breaks curfew and the next day they want to take the car to school, simply remind them of your agreement that they needed to be home by a certain time or the car would not be available the next day which is today. I do not have to go on and on about their lack of discipline or not keeping their word. (I can mention these without belaboring them). In fact, I will sound encouraging by telling him, "not today, but tomorrow you should be able to borrow it." Do not take this to mean that when they got home late last night, you did not ask for an explanation. Additionally, I am not stating that if violating curfew has become a problem, the discipline may not need to be more severe or the conversation with them lengthier. However, less is best still applies here.

If the lights are left on in a room, no need to talk about the price of electricity or their irresponsibleness. Parents, I assume you have probably talked about both of these issues already. Simply use three words, "Kids, the lights." If a child is running out the door and is forgetting his lunch on the breakfast table, "son, your lunch" may be sufficient. Yes, we feel like telling a child who keeps forgetting things that if his head was not attached to his neck, he would forget it.

Our children and teens especially have more energy than we do. They will argue in hopes that we will say, "OK, take the car, but you better be home on time today or forget about ever driving my car." Alas, I just said something that I will probably never follow up on (never to allow them to drive my car), thus further eroding their respect for me as a parent. Giving in erodes our children's respect for us.

I should also mention that it is not good to pile on complaints. Deal with the rule violation and refrain from the statement, "and another thing." In other words, deal with one issue at a time and deal with the issue when it occurs. Many times, when we are handing out discipline, we remember that we have let other misbehaviors slide, so we pile on. This brings out the need to deal with a misbehavior when it occurs, and not disciplining when we are simply overwhelmed with numerous issues.

Statements such as, "You better put your toys away or else" or "I am only telling you one more time," are draining on a parent. Train your children to know that when you tell them that it is time to put the toys away you will only give the order once. If the order is not obeyed the first time, a consequence occurs such as parents immediately picking up the toys and sending the child to their room. Not allowing them to play with certain toys the next day may also be appropriate. Again, no need to lecture, yell, or tell the child how upset they have made you. Just give the consequence.

Related to less is best, parents need to major on the majors and ignore as much as possible the minors. By this, I mean that there is a tendency in all parents to pick on our children for every little thing that is wrong. I hear parents constantly telling their children to stand up straight, tuck their shirt tails in, not to talk with their mouths full, etc. etc. Yes, I know we want children to know socially acceptable behavior, but my thought here is that when we nitpick about everything, we (and our children) are too worn out to sit and talk when a serious issue needs to be addressed.

So, less is best. Do not be overwhelmed, parents; with God's help and grace, you are becoming amazing parents!

CHAPTER TEN

FINDING OUT WHAT LOVE IS TO THEM

There are wonderful books in our bookstores about the love languages of our children. It is not difficult finding out what is love to them. In their book *The Five Love Languages for Children*, Gary Chapman and Ross Campbell encourage parents to observe how our children communicate love to us. Furthermore, pay attention to what they complain about not getting from you (i.e., you never have time to play with me), and when given a choice between two activities, observe which one they choose.

The issue is to realize that the inner needs for love that our children have will only be met when we communicate love to them in ways that make them <u>feel</u> loved. This is perhaps an extreme example, and maybe it is not. Men, you can take your daughter to a ballgame, or you can have an imaginary tea time with her toy tea set. The issue here is to find out which one she prefers. Maybe your girl <u>would</u> prefer a ballgame.

All children like gifts, yet I would dare to say that most children would exchange some toys for a hug or two from mom or dad. Some would even exchange their expensive toys for mom and dad to play with them. It is also important to remind parents that though many of our children's needs remain the same as they grow older, some will change with time.

It is painful to hear a parent state, "but I love my child" when told that their son or daughter does not feel loved by them. I remember hearing an internationally known minister say years ago that the Lord told him, "Your son thinks that you think he is a bad boy." The minister was shocked because he did not feel this way about his son. However, the son confessed later to his father that he did think that about his dad, because of the way he had been misbehaving.

I wonder what our children think we think about them. More on this later, but how tragic when a parent truly loves a child, but the child does not <u>feel</u> loved by the parent. You may be a very affectionate parent (this is great of course), but as much as your child loves your hugs and kisses, he or she wants you to play with them. Here we have two great ways our children feel loved, physical touch and play (quality) time. Of course, all children desire time from their parents, but doing what? Perplexed? Don't be. Listen to your children. You also have the Holy Spirit to help you. He was sent to teach you all things including parenting, and He is amazing, like you!

CHAPTER ELEVEN

❖

YOU ARE AN AMAZING PARENT

Years ago, I worked in a drug rehabilitation program. Part of my responsibilities was to teach a parenting class for parents who had had their children removed from their homes due to the parent's drug use. I will never forget one parent who, in addition to being in my class, was in individual and parent/child counseling with me. This mother was quite dedicated to her recovery and to get her children back. I will never forget Rosa. I was led to tell her one day that she was a good parent. She broke down and told me that no one had ever told her that. Rosa had beaten herself enough for two people for losing her children.

I cannot say that my words to her turned her life around since she was already turning it around. However, I believe that she never forgot these words. She graduated from our program got her kids back and continued in recovery. I was not minimizing her drug use, just like Jesus did not minimize the adultery of the woman in John chapter 8. In both cases, the women simply needed grace. Grace changes people.

I have interjected this chapter in the middle of the book to give you a recess. Sit back for a minute and accept that you are a good parent. Did I say perfect? Of course, not. You should never strive for perfection but strive to forgive yourself when you fail. Let me give you a secret. We will all make mistakes at one time or another. Ok, so it was not a secret. What helps us continue to move forward is accepting that we are forgiven. Let me say it again that there is no condemnation to those in Christ Jesus.

Let me share a small Bible lesson here. Chapters 9 and 10 of the book of Hebrews talk about the perfection of our conscience (verses 6-9 in chapter 9 and verses 1- 2 in chapter 10). Interesting. The perfection God is looking for in us is not perfection in behavior but perfection in conscience. This is a conscience free from sin consciousness and condemnation. This actually leads to better behavior and parenting.

In one of my parenting classes, a parent once told me that there are no bad parents, only badly informed parents. Trust me, it sounds poetic in Spanish. I also did classes in this second language of mine. Well, I liked what she said, even though I have to admit that there are some parents in prison for hurting their children.

But if you are reading this book, have gotten this far and have a desire to help your children succeed, even if you are incarcerated, you are an amazing parent. Make use of the resources that may be available where you are. Study this book. Do not be too quick to ask them to forgive you. They may need to share the pain caused by your incarceration, so listen and acknowledge their pain. Let Jesus lift you up, accept His forgiveness, and reach out to them. Even if they do not respond, keep praying for them and reaching out to them - not for your benefit, but theirs. Do not lose hope.

Before I finish this chapter, I need to encourage all parents to take the time to nurture themselves. This is something that needs to be intentional as with everything in this book. The balance here is that as important as parenting is, allowing the entire home or marriage to revolve around the children is counterproductive. I always encourage couples to take time once a week to go out by themselves. Couples who take time to nurture one another are ultimately the best parents. A parent who does not nurture him or herself or is not nurtured by the other parent has nothing to give to the children. Parenting can be draining, in case you have not noticed.

Time alone with the Lord is still the greatest way to care for ourselves. However, regular walks, reading or whatever restful activities work for you need to be done. You can make time to rest and nurture yourself, because you are an amazing parent!

CHAPTER TWELVE

LISTEN

Yes, yes, I know we want them to listen to <u>us</u>. So, guess what? We need to model it. Grace listens, and grace does not interrupt. When they have a question, never let them think that you are too busy for them and that they are a disturbance in your life.

Of course, as parents, we need our own time to rest, so if they are interrupting something more important than them (tongue in cheek, of course), we can give them our undivided attention while we explain to them that as soon as we are done, we will get back to them. Then keep your word.

Listening has to do more with listening for the feelings than the exact content. When children complain that you do not have time to play with them, do not remind them of the time last month or last week when you played all day with them. Simply acknowledge that they desire more play time with mom or dad, and then tell them when you will be able to do it. And say it enthusiastically.

The entire parable of the sower in Mark chapter four discusses how important it is to hear the Word. Proverbs

4:20-22 is a favorite passage in the lives of many students of the Bible because it emphasizes the value of listening to the Word of God. Why not read it slowly today and see these verses as the benefits of listening to your children. As we listen to the Word of God, it brings healing. It is medicine. In the same manner, as we listen to our children, healing occurs in our relationship with them. In Matthew 13:15, Jesus clearly explained the same process. Listening brings understanding and understanding brings healing when we hear God's Word <u>and</u> when we listen to our children. In other words, listening heals relationships.

Follow these simple rules. Stop what you are doing even if it is just to tell them that you will be right with them. Give them eye contact and your undivided attention (as we do with the Word). Do not interrupt but give feedback, so they know you heard and, more importantly, understood. Listening, cannot be overemphasized. As with all the tools in this book, as we listen, we are modeling our Heavenly Father. When parents constantly interrupt, lecture, and sermonize, our children will not get a picture of our Heavenly Father for the God of grace that He is.

Listening to our children helps us to be sensitive to when they want to talk. Children seldom state, "mom/dad, can we talk?" Trust the Holy Spirit to alert you when a child may be wanting to get our attention and needs to talk. For example, if my son keeps interrupting my study time in my office, it may not be too hard to figure it out that he may want to talk.

All of our children carry two imaginary tanks. One is the love tank. They constantly need to be loved and have their love needs met. As parents, we can feed them a good breakfast in the morning after a good night sleep, pray with them before they go off to school, and tell them we love them as we hug them dropping them off at school. Generally, this will cause them to get to school with their love tank full. However, our child may fail a test or be bullied by someone at school, hence, get home from school with his love tank empty and his other imaginary tank (of negative emotions) full. This secondary imaginary tank needs to be emptied, or they will act out. Many times, when our children misbehave, it is due to negative emotions that they need to release by talking them out. This is where listening comes in.

It is important that we allow our children to have and display emotions. Your children, for example, should have a right to be angry. Telling a child that is angry not to be angry is counterproductive. However, what they do with their anger IS my concern as a parent. Helping them manage their emotions is also my concern. Parents need to know that anger is not a primary emotion. Where there is anger, a child may be feeling hurt, frustrated, or perhaps even depressed. It is our job as parents to uncover what is behind the anger. In his book *How to Really Love Your Teen*, Dr. D.

Ross Campbell indicates that teaching our child to manage anger is one of our greatest tasks as parents.

The admonition in the Bible is to be angry, but sin not. To help a child deal with anger, for example, I first have to acknowledge the anger in them and listen. However, yelling, throwing objects, hitting someone, or pouting is unacceptable. Children need to know that anger and other emotions start in the mind. When we can manage our thoughts, we can manage our emotions, since emotions come from our thought patterns. Here is another area where we can trust the Holy Spirit to give us guidelines to share with our children.

As parents, somehow, we instinctively begin to give answers and solutions to our children when they talk to us about some problem. James 1:19 talks about being slow to speak and quick to listen. It even admonishes us to be slow to get angry. This verse is an excellent parenting scripture. If a child expresses having problems with math, don't be too quick to tell him how easy math is, to study more or even the need to spend less time texting. Acknowledge their feelings before venturing into giving solutions. Maybe they already know what to do and just need to vent some. In my parenting classes, I frequently address what I call "door openers." Simple phrases such as "um-hum," "tell me more," and "is that right?" open the door for our children to talk more.

If a child says it is not cold outside, do not try to convince them that it is. However, you can still mandate they wear a jacket. If they did not like the movie, do not tell them they are wrong and that the movie was awesome. It is as simple as this. Too much denying of their feelings, and they will close their hearts to us. Selah, pause and think about it.

When we respect their feelings and listen to how overwhelmed they are feeling, they will be more open to listen to our suggestions. And yet, helping them come up with their own solution to a problem is golden. By this, I mean teaching them how to ask God for wisdom and learning to be quiet to hear the Spirit of the Lord inside them. (More on this particular issue later). This works with our older children but can work with a younger child as well. Smile, parents. Hey, you are learning. You are an amazing parent!

CHAPTER THIRTEEN

———◆·❧·❁·❦·◆———

KEEP YOUR WORD

It bears repeating that our children will develop a concept of our Heavenly Father from mom and dad, but mainly from dad. If we promise something, we need to follow through. Psalm 15:4 describes the integrity of the person that swears even to his own hurt. Talk about powerful modeling. I have heard numerous times the story of a well-known minister of the gospel who shares about his father's decision to tell the truth in court, in spite of it costing him a large sum of money. This particular minister himself is known for his integrity and his absolute commitment to keep his word. Sounds like he learned something from his dad.

Our children will learn to trust the truthfulness of the Word of God when they grow up knowing that their parents kept their word to them. In other words, our children may find it hard to believe in the integrity of their Heavenly Father's Word when their earthly father or mother never kept theirs.

Talk to them if there is ever a time when you promise something and then cannot keep the promise because of unforeseen circumstances. Explain the situation and reschedule. Your children will respect you for this. I should note, however, that too much of having to reschedule with them is not good. The bottom line is for children to have absolute confidence that when we promise something, they can be assured that it is coming. Keeping our word to our children communicates to them how valuable and important they are to us.

We live in a society where breaking your word is not frowned upon like in the past. I have heard people say that transactions used to be finalized with a handshake, but now we need lengthy contracts and attorneys. Maybe this characterization is somewhat romanticized. And yet, it has some truth. One of the greatest things our children should be able to say about us when we are gone is that they could depend on our word. I could spend much time talking about the legacy we should leave behind. Actually, this is what this whole book is about.

So, what do we do if we have not always kept our word? Accept God's forgiveness, ask them to forgive you, and move on, because you are an amazing parent!

CHAPTER FOURTEEN

TEACH GRACE BY MODELING

I remember hearing a story about a father who told his son to tell the truth always. However, when he took his son to a movie, he told him to lie about his age since he was shorter than the average 12-year-old. Under 12-year old got in at half price. The issue is, what will the child remember more? What his father <u>told</u> him or what he <u>showed</u> him? The answer is easy to figure out. Not only do we talk to our children about grace and the Father's love, but we demonstrate it to them and others. This is powerful modeling. When people are not nice to you, be nice to them in front of your children.

Teach children the value of respect and honor. There are several groups that in our society are not respected as in the past. These include police officers, teachers, and parents themselves. Never talk disrespectfully about the police. Teachers and all in authority are to be addressed with Mr., Mrs., Miss, or their title, such as Mayor or officer.

In teaching grace by modeling, how couples treat one another in front of the children is extremely important.

It has been said that the greatest thing a dad can do for his children is to love their mother. I would add that the greatest thing a mom can do is respect her husband. This is a great part of helping children to grow up feeling secure, safe, and loved.

Let your children see you giving God thanks for all the good things that come into your lives. This includes the big and little things. Our children need to know that all good comes from the grace of God and not our self-efforts.

We have already addressed parents forgiving their children quickly. But what about others that the children become aware have hurt their parents in some way? We will model forgiveness as we forgive those who have not been nice to us. And encourage your children, parents, to be quick to forgive those who hurt them.

Be kind to the elderly and the people society looks down on. Be kind to little children. Be overtly thankful in front of your children to waiters and waitresses. I could go on and on. The main point is that many children remember more what they see than what we tell them. Our children are always watching us. Hence, model grace. Give unmerited, undeserved favor. You can do this, since you are an amazing parent!

CHAPTER FIFTEEN

───◆◆❖◆◆───

TRAINING UP YOUR CHILDREN IN THE WAY THEY SHOULD GO

Much has been written by scholars and Bible teachers about Proverbs 22:6. I will not argue with those who agree with the Amplified version (AMPC) that indicates that as parents we are to train up our children in keeping with their individual gift or bent. I am neither a Hebrew nor Greek scholar. I am still working on learning English.

Nonetheless, I will humbly share my thoughts on this verse. First of all, the word translated "train" in this verse is "chanak" in the Hebrew. According to the website Bible. org, Principle of Nurturing (Training Your Child), this word could mean "to dedicate," "to discipline," "instruction," and even "to initiate or create an appetite." From this insight, we can see that what we want our children to move toward, be strong in, or stay with as they grow older, we need to cultivate a taste for.

This is awesome for me in the light of grace-based parenting. In essence, we should desire all our children not just to know God, His goodness and grace, but to taste it. When they actually taste that the Lord is good, if they taste later the ways of the world, they will reject them because they have tasted better. I think I have discovered the answer to the big question many pastors and parents have had for years. It is the question as to why through the years we have lost so many of our youths when they grow up and leave home.

I believe that most of our children and youth (and most adults too) have been taught a mixture of law and the grace of God. Yes, they have been taught that the Lord is good, but at the same time that His will may not be to heal them, that He will punish them for their sins, and that, though they may have been saved by grace, they need to perform to stay right with God. There are many other statements I could add to that list. Therefore, they have been taught a mixture, but have never tasted pure grace, the goodness of God.

David stated in Psalm 34:8 to taste that the Lord is good. In 1 Peter 2:2-3 Peter indicates that we will grow by spending time in the Word of God, "if indeed you have tasted that the Lord is gracious." We all want our children to spend time reading the Bible. It will not be a chore to them (and us) if they taste. Taste does not mean to preach to them the laws and regulations, but to have them experience the goodness of God. Parents, when you experience the goodness of God, share it with them. As parents get a revelation of God's love for them, our children will see it in our lives. They will see that for mom and dad, Christianity is not a set of rules, but a relationship with our Great God and Savior, Jesus. As the old song says, "Oh, what a Savior!"

The phrase "he should go" comes from the Hebrew word "Pei," which means mouth. Hence, we could say "in the way of their mouth." We are to train, then, by cultivating a taste for the goodness of God. This is just like giving your little one's vegetables so they will acquire a taste for them. Additionally, we are to train them by helping them to speak only words of grace and faith. Our children need to learn how to talk. I am not simply referring to swear words, but any word that does not speak of the goodness and grace of God or any word lacking in faith.

All the chapters in this book point to how to give our children a taste of the grace of God. Relax, parents, this is not all that hard. Remember that His grace is available to help you grow. You are an amazing parent!

CHAPTER SIXTEEN

PRAY THE WORD

First and foremost, pray that they will experientially encounter the goodness and grace of God. Pray that the eyes of their understanding will be opened to see the goodness of God. Therefore, pray, but also talk to them constantly about how good Jesus is and what He has done for us. This is the principle in Deuteronomy 6:7 applied to the new covenant.

Most parents know to pray for their children, but what is needed is to pray the Word of God over them. For example, Proverbs chapter 2:1-4 can be prayed in this manner using the NKJV translation:

Father, I declare in Jesus' name that my children receive Your words and treasure Your commands within them. They incline their ear to wisdom and apply their heart to understanding. They cry out for discernment and lift up their voice for understanding. They seek wisdom as they would seek silver and search for her as for hidden treasure.

This is just an example. Many verses can be prayed over them such as Isaiah 54:13, Matthew 6:33, Psalm 112:2(a),

Matthew 5:6, Psalm 127:3-4, and Proverbs 10:1(a). The idea is to personalize the verses.

Never pray the problem, pray the answer. Job prayed his fears and prayed the problem. Unknowingly, he opened the door to the thief that Jesus talked about in John 10:10. And, no, it was not God who gave Satan permission to attack Job. Job himself stated in Job 3:25 that the thing he feared had come upon him. In Job 1:12 God was merely pointing out to the devil that Job had already placed himself in the devil's hands through his fears. Never pray your fears by telling God that you worry about calamity coming on your children or that you fear them turning their back on Him.

There are many areas that parents need to pray regarding their children. Pray that God brings godly friends to them but removes the ungodly. Pray even when they are young that they will discover and answer the call of God on their lives, that they will make right decisions regarding their education, dating and eventually marriage.

If concerned about their safety, speak Psalm 91 over them. Never declare anything but your faith when asked how they are doing. If they are going through a tough time remember that you owe no one an explanation when asked how they are doing. You can merely state, "Thanks for asking how my children are doing. They are disciples taught by the Lord and great is their peace." This is the promise of God in Isaiah 54:13. Of course, you can ask a person knowledgeable of the Bible to agree with you in prayer as Matthew 18:19 indicates.

Speak that your children honor you. Declare that you have favor with them and that they will live long on the earth. And again, when asked about them, never declare anything contrary to what you have been declaring in the presence of God every morning. I love Psalm 145:9. I speak that God's tender mercies; His goodness and grace are over your children and you today. And in keeping with the title of this book, pray for their eyes to be opened to God's love and His unmerited and undeserved favor. Yes, you are an amazing parent!

CHAPTER SEVENTEEN

◆◈◆✳◆◈◆

SPEAK GRACE OVER YOUR CHILDREN

This chapter continues with the previous chapter on praying the Word over your children. Let's talk about specifically speaking grace over our children. Ephesians 4:29 commands us to let no corrupt communication leave our mouth, but only to speak grace. Only speak grace over your children when you pray for them, as well as when you speak to them and about them. We have defined grace as the unearned, undeserved favor of God. This changes most of the things we have been saying over our children. Let me give you some specific grace–based prayer.

2 Corinthians 13:14: Father, I speak the grace of our Lord Jesus Christ, the love of God and the communion of the Holy Spirit over my children.

Galatians 1:3: I speak grace, your unmerited favor over them as well as your peace, nothing missing, and nothing broken in their lives. I believe that whatever is missing, you supply it to them. Whatever is broken, you fix.

1 Peter 4:10: I declare that the gift (grace) that they have received from You, they minister it to others and use it for the glory of Your name.

Colossians 4:6: I believe that all their speech is with grace. All their speech ministers God's grace, His undeserved favor to others.

Galatians 2:21, (KJV): They do not frustrate the grace of God but recognize that righteousness comes only by faith and not through the law. They receive abundance of grace and the gift of righteousness daily (Romans 5:17). Therefore, they reign over sin, bad habits and addictions.

Romans 6:14: Sin does not have dominion over them because they are no longer under the law but grace.

2 Corinthians 9:8: All grace is abounding toward them.

I could go on and on. As with our ultimate goal in parenting (chapters 3 and 4), we want our children to receive a revelation of the grace of God. The grace of God is truly the gospel of the Lord Jesus Christ which brought in the new and better covenant. The new covenant is amazing, and so are you!

CHAPTER EIGHTEEN

◆❖◆

AVOID PLACING YOURSELVES AND YOUR CHILDREN UNDER THE LAW

It has been alluded to already, but parents need to avoid placing themselves and their children under the law. For parents, statements such as, "I am such a terrible parent" or "why did I mess up again" are not grace statements. Anytime you condemn yourself, you have placed yourself under the law. These statements place demands on us. Remember that the law demands (thou shall not, thou shall not, thou shall not), but grace supplies. When we are under grace we are not need-minded (the "I have to" statements), but cognizant of the help grace supplies. Our Father does not want us relying on our own strength, but on His grace, which He abundantly supplies daily.

We place our children under the law when we are legalistic, demand perfection from them and things from them that we are not willing to do ourselves. Avoid correction without grace or placing their obedience to rules above your relationship with them, above communicating to them your love and God's mercy, love, and grace. If all our relationship and communication with our children is based on "do not do this" or "do not do that" you can then understand why Paul stated our children can be provoked to anger. Some people think that is what Christianity is all about—"do not do this" and "do not do that."

As much as possible, avoid statements such as, "I demand you respect me" or "I demand you obey the rules." I <u>expect</u> you to obey and respect me is better because ultimately demanding respect is not grace. Respect is earned. Yes, I know our children are told in the Bible to honor their parents. The implication is that they are to honor even if a parent is not respectful toward them. Nonetheless, it is best to command respect by our modeling of grace, being consistent in discipline, and everything else mentioned in this book. Grace loves and earns the respect of others. However, a lack of respect on the part of your children needs to be addressed.

I heard a great man once say that some things are best caught than taught. Grace-based parenting is like that. Pray that God will teach you more and more His love for you and how to communicate with grace to your children. Why not remind them about some behavior we desire from them, rather than the behavior we do not desire from them. If parents were honest with themselves, they would admit that they spend much time of the day with statements such as, "<u>Stop</u> hitting your sister," "<u>stop</u> slurping your soup," "<u>stop</u>

slouching," and on and on. Remember that the old covenant which (included the 10 commandments) was mostly about what behavior was NOT acceptable.

Above all, a key issue is how we see our children. If we see them as burdens, we will become law-based. If we resist the thoughts to see them in this manner, we can then communicate in grace. Work on casting down the negative thoughts (2 Corinthians 10:3-5) that the devil brings to you about your poor parenting or the negative thoughts about your children getting in the way, being burdens or that they will never change. In essence, how we see our children will determine if we see them as tasks (law) or rewards (grace) from the Lord (Psalm 127:3).

I am not saying parenting is not work but look at it this way. How do we see tithing, going to church, or reading our Bible? If we see them as tasks, we have to do every day rather than things we get to do, these things will be yokes around our necks. These things under grace are things that flow out of our revelation of His great love and forgiveness and an understanding that where the Old Covenant was all about demands the new is all about supply. Relax, parents. Whatever parenting issues come up during the day God has it covered. His supply is already there giving us the wisdom, strength, and grace to deal with the situations. I believe all grace is abounding toward you (2 Corinthians 9:8).

Do not take away from this chapter that we do not have rules for our children. Rules protect. Placing them under law is again, demanding perfection, correcting without grace, and having rules about every little thing in life. Remember that the law in the old testament demanded perfection. The book of James states that if one law was broken then, in essence, we were breaking them all. I am not stating that there are no consequences for violating a rule only that having rules about everything and never giving grace when even the smallest rule is broken can lead to our children being provoked to anger (Ephesians 6:4).

They will feel that no matter how many of our rules they keep we are not pleased with them until they keep all of them. Many times, it is not what we correct but HOW we do it. It bears repeating here that our children need to know we approve of them and are pleased with them without them having to obey all the rules. No, this does not mean that we are never firm with our children. Hey, do not get stressed out. You are an amazing parent!

CHAPTER NINETEEN

◆▸▷◈◁◂◆

SPIRIT LED GRACE-BASED PARENTING

A s an introduction to this chapter, I need to remind you of one of the articles of the new covenant as noted in Hebrews 8:8-12. In the new covenant, God no longer writes His laws in tablets of stone, but in our hearts. First of all, believe that the Spirit of God desires to guide you in your day-to-day parenting. The Holy Spirit knows everything about everything (John 14:26), including parenting. No one parenting book can tell you what to do in every single situation. Secondly, we need to encourage our children to believe that as born-again Christians, God speaks to them and they can hear Him. This will help our children make godly decisions in all areas, especially in hearing the call of God on their lives, the church He has for them to attend, and be committed to as well as decisions regarding dating and marriage.

What happens when your teenager comes in late from curfew? He should accept a consequence for this depending on how late he stayed out. Suppose he profusely apologizes, and you sense a need to let it go, honestly believing that he lost track of time. Another time say that he stopped to help someone out and got home half an hour late. I cannot tell you what to do, so you need to listen to the Spirit of God. Trust God that He is for you and witnesses to you what to do.

Do not expect to hear an audible voice although this can happen. Most of the time God leads by the inner witness (Romans 8:16) which is simply an inner knowing. Sometimes we call it a hunch or an inner impression. God even puts desires in our hearts that are intended to guide us. John 16:13 and John 14:26 show us emphatically that the Spirit of God does speak to us. Furthermore, Jesus stated that His sheep DO hear His voice in John 10:27.

As our children constantly hear from us how much the Father and Jesus love them and learn the beauties of our Savior, the result will be wanting to spend time with our Lord. This is doing "the one thing" that Jesus told Martha that her sister had chosen. Our children do not necessarily need to learn every single step to hearing from God. They will hear from Him as they enjoy His presence, bask in His love, and rest that when they need to be directed in any area, He will speak.

Learn to listen to the Spirit of God inside. You can talk to Him, and He will respond. The spirit of man is the lamp of the Lord (Proverbs 20:27). He uses our spirits to guide us.

Most Christians have never learned this, and instead let the circumstances dictate to them what they <u>feel</u> God is telling them to do. However, God does not lead us by our feelings (which can lie to us) or by the natural circumstances. It is not biblically correct to be led by circumstances, since Romans 8:14 shows us that it is by His Spirit that God wants to lead us. Nor is it correct to put a fleece out for the Lord. That is how God led people in the Old Testament when the Spirit of God did not live in His people.

Remember Romans 8:26 states that when we do not know how to pray, the Spirit of God is there to help us pray in the spirit for our children. Thank you, Jesus, for the gift of being able to pray supernaturally even when we do not know in the natural what is going on with our children. And finally, thank God that the Holy Spirit desires to reveal to us when they are having problems or facing temptations. He will even show us things to come in the lives of our children (John 16:13). Parents, you have supernatural help and can parent supernaturally since you are amazing parents!

CHAPTER TWENTY

TIME TO PLAY

Yes, I know, everything takes time. It seems we never seem to have enough time in 24 hours to do all we need to do. If only we did not have to sleep. But alas, until we get our glorified bodies, we will have to sleep. Should I rephrase that statement and say we <u>get to sleep?</u>

As Bible believers, we need to believe what God says. Proverbs 3:2 promises length of days. This is not living many years. That is another promise (Psalm 91:16). Length of days has to do with God giving us more than enough time to do what we need to do and desire to do every day.

I read recently about a study that found that there is little correlation between how much time parents spend with their children and how they turn out. However, the scriptures tell us that a child left to oneself is destructive (Proverbs 29:15). A key issue here is uninterrupted face-to-face contact with your children. Parents start with the amount of time you can give your child and I promise you that you will find yourself with more and more time to spend with them. Many ask which is most important, quality or quantity time? My answer is both. However, do not allow condemnation if at times you do not have all the time to spend with them that you desire. Some parents may need to put time with the children on their calendars or time with them will never happen.

Regarding play, most parents do not realize the social, physical and even spiritual benefits of play time. Getting out to the yard or park to play has its own benefits. Emotionally, children connect with us in their playtime and learn many things such as how to manage their emotions (nobody likes to lose, right, parents?). Playtime develops character in our children like good sportsmanship, honor (giving honor to the person who defeated you), and perseverance. However, men, not all playtime has to be competitive.

On top of all this, our children learn we value them when we make time to play with them. How great it is to laugh and be joyful with them. Some people grew up thinking that God hates it when we play because their parents never played with them or looked down on leisure time. Relax parents. God likes it when we take time to play and relax. Playing with our children and grandchildren reminds us not to take life so seriously.

Let me finish with what could be a chapter in and of itself. Make time for their little league games, school programs, and any event they would like you to attend. Can we attend them all? Maybe not, but remember that they will grow up, and they do grow up fast. Do not miss the opportunities before you, because you are an amazing parent!

CHAPTER TWENTY-ONE

———◆ ❖ ◆———

A NOTE TO THE LOCAL CHURCH

It will take the whole body of Christ working together to save our children. Someone stated that it would take a village, but I do not want my neighbor across the street who is not a Christian or even an ungodly school teacher raising my children. As a pastor, I am responsible for communicating to my church that they all have some responsibility in the raising of our church's children. I am not just talking about Sunday School or youth department. This is great, but in a local church, every member of that church is responsible to some degree to encourage our children, tell them that they are loved, and that they are champions. Church members should never complain about the amount of money invested by the church in our children and youth.

Single parents are especially in need of the body of a local church coming together to help them. Men can take time with the children of these single moms since they may have no healthy males in their lives. In the Old Testament, we read that King David's uncles served as his advisors. I am an uncle and great uncle to many nephews and nieces. It is my responsibility to communicate acceptance to them especially in the struggles of adolescence. This is even more important in the local church. This responsibility has not been stressed enough in our local churches. I encourage single parents to believe God to bring older mature Christians into the lives of their children.

I am not stating that we are responsible for intervening every time a single parent in your church has a serious issue with their children. However, we should be praying for the children of our local church. Furthermore, when you encounter children and youth in church, greet them as you would an adult. In other words, do not ignore them. This is the least we can do along with reminding them that God loves them and that you think they are wonderful. This is done in actions and in words. It takes the entire body of Christ which has the most amazing parents like you!

CHAPTER TWENTY-TWO

◆━◈◆✳◆◈━◆

LEAN ON THE GRACE,
"CARRY ME, PAPA"

Several years ago, my great niece who is pictured on my first book *Amazing Love* came into my life. We became very close. We used to walk to her favorite local store every week. Though able to walk (she was four by then) she would tell me "Carry me, papa." She thought I was her father, but later found out I am her great uncle. I used to give her a big "no" and remind her that she was now a big girl and could walk. But, alas, she had gotten into my heart by that time, so up into my arms she would go.

About 18 months ago, the Lord woke me up and reminded me of her saying ("carry me, papa") since I was going through a hard time in my body. Though I had never prayed like this before, I felt impressed to say to God, "Carry me, Papa." I was feeling overwhelmed. Later, I found verses in the Word of God that show that God wants to do precisely this for us, but as adults, we feel that we have to "tough it out on our own."

John 15:2 states that any branch in Jesus that does not bear fruit He takes away. A study of the Greek word translated "takes away," however, indicates that it could also be translated "He LIFTS UP." Is the traditional way we have translated this verse really in line with what we know of our Savior and His grace? Of course not. Furthermore, some fruit and vegetable plants need to be lifted up and placed on trellises to produce the best fruit and vegetables.

Remember the story in Luke 15 about the shepherd who went looking for the one lost sheep? It is such a brief but powerful story. The shepherd did not scold (do you scold sheep?) the sheep when he found it. It clearly states that he looked for it <u>until</u> he found it and then he put it on his shoulders and rejoiced. Hey, sheep, even if they are babies, are not all that light. I remember a song entitled, "Love Lifted Me" which I learned in my childhood. He wants to lift you up.

So, if you are feeling overwhelmed, let Him carry you. Ask Him to carry you. He loves you. Grace is leaning on the One inside of us and not trying to fix things with our own limited human skills and knowledge. See Deuteronomy 32:11, Isaiah 40:11, Isaiah 41:10, Isaiah 46:4, Isaiah 63:9. Let God carry you. Why not read the above-given scriptures before going on to the next chapter? You are an amazing parent, so let Him carry you!

CHAPTER TWENTY-THREE

GIRLS/BOYS, UNDERSTANDING THEIR DIFFERENT NEEDS

There are many common needs that our children have. Some are different, however, although the differences will be in degrees depending on the temperament of your children. Most girls need to feel loved, lovely and special. Boys, of course, need the same but they need to feel competent/capable as well. They need to hear what a great job they did. If you are thinking that your girls like to hear praise about their accomplishments as well, you are right.

However, I believe that most men struggle with incompetence and most women struggle with feeling loved, lovely and unique. If this was not the case Ephesians chapter 5:33 would not tell women to respect (which the Amplified Bible indicates is praise, veneration and esteeming him) their husbands. The implication is clear. Most men having never heard as children how competent and capable they were need the words of praise from their wives.

In the same vein, Ephesians 5:25-26 admonishes husbands to love their wives as Christ loved the church and to sanctify and cleanse them through his words. The Message Translation of these same verses' states that the love of Christ and His words makes us whole and <u>evokes our beauty</u>. As husbands love their wives as Christ loves the church their words evoke the beauty of their wives. The implication is clear. Wives need to feel loved, lovely, and precious, since as little girls most were not treated as loved, lovely, and precious. And by the way, the world does not treat men as competent either. Listen to most sitcoms, and you will find this out. And the world does not treat our girls and women as precious and the equal of men. Only the Bible, the new covenant, does.

Not every girl will be a cheerleader, homecoming queen, or the valedictorian, but every girl needs to feel special to her parents just the way she is. Not every boy will be the star in sports or be accepted into West Point, but all need to feel that they are capable. Of course, both need to hear the joy that having them in our lives brings to us.

Have you ever read how in the Bible so many men God called did not feel capable to do what God assigned them to do? Let's start with Moses, Gideon, Saul, and Jeremiah. I know David, Joshua, and Caleb come to mind as men who felt competent, but you will find such men in the minority. Jeremiah told God that he was but a youth. Moses reminded

God that he was a stutterer. Saul hid when time to anoint him king, and Gideon called himself the least in his father's family.

And how many women in the Bible do you hear not accepting their uniqueness and value? Even Mary had a problem when the angel called her blessed and highly favored. I am not saying this is always the case, but keep this in mind, parents, girls who realize they are loved, lovely, and precious due to their parents' words and actions develop healthy relationships with the opposite sex. Much female promiscuity is due to girls searching for the love they never got from their fathers. Boys who feel competent generally avoid acting rebellious and resisting authority. They will not go to either extreme of being prideful or feeling incompetent.

Do not leave this chapter thinking that boys do not like being told that they are handsome and that girls do not like "high fives." I am just stating two great needs in our children – to feel loved, lovely and unique (girls) and to feel competent (boys). Let the Holy Spirit teach you how to meet these two needs in your children. And remember the other steps in this book since they point to the needs of our children as well.

In our present society, there is a trend to blur the differences between sexes. Therefore, it needs to be emphasized that boys need to be allowed to be boys and girls the same. Yes, our boys can grow up being more sensitive but not feminized. Girls can play the same sports the boys play, but the uniqueness and difference of girls still need to be emphasized. Our sons need to learn from their fathers how precious females are, how they are different from boys and how to treat them. Girls need to learn how boys think, and how they are also different not just sexually but psychologically.

Fathers are to date their daughters, so they can learn how a male is to treat them. Additionally, girls need to learn from dads how to protect themselves from males that only want to use them for sex. As dad treats mom like a queen, our sons will see modeled how to treat a woman. Much can be said in this area, but for more information, I recommend the books *That's my Girl* and *That's my Son* by Rick Johnson. And yet, trust the Holy Spirit in preparing our sons to be men of honor and our young ladies women of virtue.

And finally, in communicating God's love and our love to our children, we will help our girls and boys not to base their sense of value on their beauty, their accomplishments or their physical prowess but on God's love for them and their identity in Christ. Outward beauty fades as well as physical strength. Basing their sense of value on accomplishments can be devastating when failures occur. Therefore, above all keep teaching and telling your children how totally unconditional Jesus' love is and keep loving them just the way they are every day. You can do it since you are an amazing parent!

CHAPTER TWENTY-FOUR

UNDERSTANDING THEIR TEMPERAMENTS

Not only are boys and girls different but the temperaments of our children will all be different. Praise the Lord for this. It would be boring if all our children were the same. Before going further in this chapter never compare temperaments by saying, "I wish you were more like…" Furthermore, remember that the child with the temperament more like you may rub you the wrong way more than the others.

Some children are more sociable. Some like to spend more time by themselves and play putting things together and taking them apart. Encourage the latter to be courteous around people and to be sociable but do not push. The former may need to learn to spend time alone by themselves and the Lord. Life is balance.

I believe John and Peter were very different in their temperaments. Peter was probably more self-confident (dare I say prideful) and John definitely more sociable. But both were loved the same by the Master, and both were used by Him in establishing the church. Peter was a trailblazer along with Paul. John was the Apostle of love and undoubtedly a great encourager to the church. Their different temperaments and callings were used by God in different ways.

Never excuse bad behavior as "Well, that is how they are." My point in this brief chapter is to understand that our children will be different, and we must recognize this. There is not one better temperament. All temperaments need to be molded by God, by His grace and love. Peter's pride and temperament had to be molded to develop humility, but he was still Peter until his death.

So, what do we do as parents? We have already covered this. Communicate the love of and the grace of God to all your children. Then as you spend time with God and the Holy Spirit, they will show you where to help all your children reach a balance in their lives that will bring God glory.

Remember that accepting their temperament does not mean ignoring negative behavior. This is not what I am talking about. Some children are probably like me. I am quite happy spending all afternoon with a book or two and a fruit smoothie. But I need to get out at times and meet with other pastors who can sharpen my skills and calling. I think you get the point since you are an amazing parent!

CHAPTER TWENTY-FIVE

◆ ⋯✦⋯ ◆

THE ULTIMATE DESIRE FOR PARENTS

Now that we have discussed the ultimate goal (chapters 3 and 4) in parenting, let me talk with you about the number one desire we have for our children. This may surprise you, but the number one thing that we want from our children is to have a relationship with them. From there, we will then lead them to have a relationship with God. You don't agree? Well, think about our Heavenly Father. Most people believe that the number one thing God desires from us is our obedience. I disagree. I believe that the number one thing God desires from us in the new covenant is to have a relationship with us. How many times have we heard preachers (and maybe yourself as well) say that Christianity is not a religion, but it is about a relationship and a relationship with Jesus and God Himself. Maybe we should believe this.

Of course, God wants obedience, but is this the number one thing? When we develop a relationship with Him, from the relationship we have with Him, obedience (transformation from the heart and not just outward modification) will flow. This is what God wants from us, and we want from our children. When I say relationship with our Father and our Lord Jesus, I am referring to obtaining a revelation of His love and grace. It is about spending time with Him around the Word of God, and to come daily to Him to receive more and more from Him and grow in the knowledge of His love for us.

Let's think about two children in the same family. One child is very obedient. In fact, he rarely if ever breaks the house rules. The other is still a good kid but tends to violate rules once in a while. However, he loves to spend time with dad and mom. He may be a good listener who enjoys listening to dad and mom talk about their own childhood. When he breaks a rule, he always recognizes it, apologizes and still enjoys time with both parents. The other child who is better behaved keeps to himself and rarely seems to enjoy family time. He behaves well because he has never been convinced of his parents' love. He may be trying to earn his parents' love via obedience. Think such a home does not exist? Well, I have just described what could have very well been the prodigal son's family.

The story in the 19th chapter of Luke closes when the prodigal returns home and the older son resents the welcome the younger son gets. The older son was more obedient. The younger son came home, and I believe formed a close relationship with his dad. I do not believe the older son ever did.

Trust me, parents, when I say that you want a relationship with your children, not just their obedience. <u>From the relationship, however, will come the obedience, but not necessarily the other way around</u>. What happens many times is as parents we tend to spend all our time on getting our children to follow the rules and never develop a relationship with them. Therefore, lasting change (inner transformation) does not occur.

If our children are to embrace from the heart our biblical values relationship with them becomes the priority. This is what God desires from us - heart change, not just outward obedience. Outward obedience (to avoid the consequences) was what the people did in the Old Testament. In my parenting classes, I always talk about the first law of parenting. Rules with no relationship bring rebellion. This is the RRR rule.

So, what do we do to develop a relationship? Well, that is what this whole book is about. A key verse is Ephesians 5:1 in the Amplified Bible, which states that we are to imitate God as well-beloved children imitate their father. The more we recognize that we are well-beloved, the more we follow or imitate God. The implication is clear. The more our children recognize that we love them, the more they will imitate us, and in imitating us, the Lord Jesus.

I will repeat what I have stated several times. I am not stating that we eliminate the rules. We simply prioritize relationship. Stay with me. I will talk more about this in the next chapter. You are an amazing parent!

CHAPTER TWENTY-SIX

◆•✦•◆

ADDING GRACE TO RULES, DISCIPLINE AND GIVING CONSEQUENCES

Bible-based parenting is built on grace. A verse parents need to know is Proverbs 16:21. This verse talks about the sweetness of lips increasing learning. The truth is that many times it is not what we say to our children, but how we say it. Colossians 4:6 admonishes us that our speech should always be with grace. Ephesians 4:29 states the same thing, adding the importance of our words always ministering grace to our hearers. I love the Message translation that states that each word we speak should be a gift. Really, every chapter in this book lays the groundwork to issue rules with grace and discipline with grace.

So, with grace, we correct. All discipline and correction need to end with reminding our children of our love for them and God's love. Additionally, rules need to be given with grace. Avoid threatening your children. I know that in the Old Testament we hear God issuing warnings to His people. Warnings are good. Threats can provoke our children to anger (Ephesians 6:4) Therefore, avoid the "you better not do it again or else" or the "do it one more time and see what happens."

Parents give your children a choice but do not threaten. For example, if a child is misbehaving in the living room as the family is playing together or watching a movie, state that you expect them to stop bothering their siblings or be excused to their room. If the child continues to be disruptive, no need to yell, "OK, I told you what would happen." Simply in a normal tone, advise them they have <u>made a choice</u> and can now go to their room and read.

To give another example, if a teen breaks a curfew, they should already know what the consequence will be. Parents should discuss this with their teens once they start going out. If they break the curfew rule, don't yell, just remind them what the consequence is per your previous talks with them. Of course, you want to know what happened, why they came home late. This does not do away with what I shared in chapter 19. It just adds another tool to parenting.

Later, communicate to your child your love and reiterate your expectations without rehashing the whole incident again. I could call this chapter choices and consequences. In grace, we give them a choice or choices and then tell them what the consequence will be if a rule is broken. This is empowering to your children. Instead of threats, we tell them that they have a choice. If they disobey, we simply tell them that they made a choice and give them the consequence.

Regarding spanking, spanking IS Biblical. However, parents must avoid using it exclusively as the only tool. Spanking should not be abused. There is a designated place to spank. My take on studies that show that spanking is counterproductive is this. Do it right, parents. The Bible is not against it, so it must be right. My belief is that if done right it leads to right results. Doing it right is never doing it out of anger or to get even. And after doing it, communicate your love. Be led by the Holy Spirit in this area. After a certain age, spanking is counterproductive. The Lord will tell you when to stop spanking.

Since this chapter discusses discipline, do not let them eat all they want and spend all their time watching TV or playing video games. Graciously limit their time watching TV. Furthermore, you approve the shows they can watch. Computers and similar devices can present a problem. Hence, parents should consider having all computers and similar devices in the living room. Too many temptations, folks.

It is good to turn off all cell phones, iPads, and similar devices sometime after dinner unless needed for homework. Our children should not go to bed texting. I think parents know their children best, so these are just suggestions. Nonetheless, with computers and similar devices in the bedrooms, how can we know what our children are seeing and doing? And, yes, I know trust is a need of our children as I already mentioned. If our children ask why we do not trust them, the simple answer is that we do not trust the flesh, theirs and ours.

Finally, I will leave you with what I heard a great pastor say once. We punish criminals, but we discipline children. I could add we give our children choices and consequences. Yes, I know our children see the consequences as punishment, but later they will realize they were not. So, parents, discipline, but do not punish to get even with them. Relax, this is not that difficult since through the grace of God you are an amazing parent!

CHAPTER TWENTY-SEVEN

❖❖❖

SMILE, PARENTS

arents, do you believe that when God looks at you, He actually smiles at you? Think about it. Numbers 6:25 in the New Living Translation and Message Bible state that God smiles on you. This is included in the priestly blessings of Numbers 6:22-27. Parents, when we believe God smiles on us and favors us, then we can treat our children in the same way. Remember Matthew 3:17 where God called Jesus His Beloved Son in whom He was well pleased. If you have received His Son Jesus Christ as your Savior, then God is well pleased with you too. God is no longer angry at us nor holding our sins against us (Isaiah 54:9; 2 Corinthians 5:19). Therefore, God is smiling at us.

For many years, I have told parents in my parenting classes to greet their children when they come home. Lately, I realized how important smiling at our children is. Of course, when they are being corrected, I do not expect parents to smile at them. However, even then, why frown so much? Smile at them when you pick them up at school, get home from school, or come to the kitchen to eat their breakfast. Smiling communicates value, approval, and warmth. I appreciate going to an office or restaurant and being greeted with a smile.

I have heard that it takes more muscles to frown than to smile. This appears to not be true, but since we usually smile more than frown, the smiling muscles are in better shape. Therefore, it takes less effort to smile. And it is true that smiling at someone is more likely to bring out a smile in the other person. Smiling further communicates to our children that they are welcomed in our lives and that they are special. Remember the first time you saw your little ones at birth? You smiled effortlessly. God smiles at us effortlessly!

When children make a request from us, we tend to frown effortlessly, since many times they do seem to interrupt us. It is important, however, to make an effort to not communicate to them that they are a hindrance in our lives. Hey, smile, parents, you are amazing parents. God smiles at you!

CHAPTER TWENTY-EIGHT

MY CHILDREN ARE OUT OF THE HOUSE

It seems that they just came home from the hospital when they start getting ready to leave home. Trust me, parents, we want them to leave home. Leaving home is good for them to do BEFORE they get married. Living on their own is a good developmental stage before marriage.

When they leave home and even when they live as adults in our home parenting changes focus. When our children are living at home as adults, we still set the rules as parents, but rules change as they grow older and mature. My emphasis in this chapter is to be thoughtful that we do not continue to treat them as children when they are now young adults. And as they move out on their own, we even let them make all of their own decisions. By then, their decisions are their own.

Hopefully, by then we have taught them how to pray, that they can hear the Spirit of God, to acknowledge Him in all their ways and how to make proper decisions. However, depending on the relationship you have developed with your children advice can be given when it is asked for. Nonetheless, it is best to be quick to listen and slow to give solutions unless impressed by the Spirit of God. Generally, it is best to help them (with the help of the Lord) come up with their own solutions to their problems.

I need to emphasize in this chapter, however, that when our children leave home much of what they have needed from us never changes. They still need words of encouragement and hugs. Of course, we can't (and should not) visit them every day. As our children were growing up, they needed grace, and they will continue to need it.

What if, as adults, they buy a car above their ability to pay for it or make a sizeable wrong investment? Well, do not get on their case. As a general rule, encourage them, and do not let them condemn themselves, but do not bail them out. Is this grace-based parenting? It is if that is what the Lord leads you to do. It is if in saying "no" you tell them "no" graciously and explain your decision without putting them down. Tell them that you trust them to hear from God as to what to do in the bind they may be in. And reiterate that God is gracious and will still help them out.

Maybe they need to learn from their actions and you bailing them out will hinder them from growing. The problem with many parents is that we do not want our children to suffer. Grace leaves them alone to learn and grow from their mistakes. What saddens me at times is finding parents still bailing out their children even when they are in their 30's and 40's.

And remember, parents, the leave and cleave rule. If they are married, they are someone else's husband or wife before being your son and daughter. Yes, I know mothers that you may still see them as your babies, but do not treat them as such. Trust me; you are still amazing parents!

CHAPTER TWENTY-NINE

CHANGE IN OUR CHILDREN AND US

Before I conclude this book, change in our children needs to be brought up again. How we get our children to change has been a question for the ages. Obviously nagging, fault-finding and even threats have had little impact through the years. Look at the people of God under the old covenant. They heard many times the consequences for serving other gods, and yet they still did. Remember the woman in John chapter eight? Even the threat of stoning did not bring change in her life. However, grace did. The gift of no condemnation did.

In reading this book, I am sure many have had the question of how our children will change if they feel no remorse for their actions. Well, I have not said that remorse is bad. Our children should feel remorse when a rule is broken, but not condemnation. Condemnation causes them to beat themselves up and keeps them stuck in the negative behavior they felt condemned for. I will reiterate that guilt, shame, and condemning statements do not bring heart change, but only temporary external behavioral modification.

2 Corinthians 3:18 is key here. We are transformed as we behold the glory of Jesus--His finished work, His grace, and His glory. Our children need to be taught the loveliness of our Savior, His finished work, and His glorious redemption. Knowing Jesus is what it is all about. That is why bringing grace into our parenting is so important. Grace (which is Jesus) changes people.

Our children need to leave our home with an understanding of how change and success in life occurs. Hard work, self-control, and sweat are not necessarily synonymous with grace. However, grace will not produce lazy kids. It will actually cause them to work harder, yet not them, but the grace of God in them (I Corinthians 15:10).

The world emphasizes hard work and discipline for getting ahead. It is time for us to emphasize grace. This is what changes our children and us. This is what our children need to understand as they leave home: that success in life can either come the world's way of relying on their skills, talents, and abilities, or the grace (His undeserved favor) of God. Otherwise, parents, when they succeed (if in fact, they do), they will give all the glory to themselves. Think about this. Additionally, they need to learn that change and growth in them will come the same way, through God's undeserved favor.

When one of our children is working on changing in some area such as overcoming an addiction or changing a bad habit, they need to be reminded that when we cannot, Jesus can. He will bring about the change in us as we lean on His undeserved favor, trust His love, and remember our identity. I like to remind people that they are loved, forgiven, and righteous. Have your children confess this every day, "I am loved, forgiven and the righteousness of God in Christ."

So many people are concerned that the preaching of grace and the love of God will lead to a lascivious lifestyle. I have yet to meet a person who truly received a revelation of how much God loved them and the finished work of Jesus, then used these truths to live like hell. If you do find someone, question if they were really saved in the first place.

However, many have been set free like the woman in John chapter eight. So, keep applying grace-based parenting. Grace and God Himself will change them. We cannot; so, relax, parents. We just provide an environment for change. To state it again, as you have prayed, trust God that He is working things out in them (Philippians 2:13).

In the story of Zacchaeus (Luke, 19th chapter), Jesus never brought out his wrong behavior. However, the grace Jesus showed him changed the man. No, I am not saying never to point out negative behavior in our children but avoid harping on them and long condemning lectures. Grace changes people. Interestingly, in the previous chapter in Luke (Luke18), Jesus encountered the rich young ruler. The young man came talking about eternal life on the merits of his own works. Jesus showed him that his own good works, (keeping of the law), could not save him. Can you see that one man was basing his life on the law and self-righteousness and no heart change occurred? Zacchaeus encountered grace, and grace changed him from the inside.

I have already stated that the goodness of God leads our children toward repentance. Understanding how much they are loved by their Heavenly Father and their true identity as Christians changes them since this is the renewing of the mind that Paul talked about in Romans 12:2. It is interesting that normally as parents we emphasize a change in behavior, when it is a change in believing and thinking that Paul was emphasizing. Right believing will bring right living.

In essence, right believing and the resulting transformation we want from our children is this. We no longer have to be after them to clean their room, eat right, or even to go to church and spend time with God. They have seen the value of cleaning their room and eating right and the beauty of spending time with the Lord. Above all, they have received a revelation that they are loved unconditionally, totally forgiven, and eternally righteous. They have changed. They have been transformed. Grace (Jesus) has changed them and will continue to change them for life.

Relax, parents. Grace (Jesus) is changing your children so do not give up, since you are amazing parents!

CHAPTER THIRTY

OBEDIENCE TO THE FAITH/ OVERCOMING TEMPTATIONS

There is so much more I think I could add to this book, but as I said previously, no one book can cover all incidents that may occur in raising our children. However, what I have attempted to do is give some grace-based principles that, along with the leading of the Holy Spirit, can lead to successful parenting.

It was a revelation to me when I discovered the difference in obedience between the old and the new covenant. Basically, the blessings of the old covenant only came when all the commandments were obeyed. In the new covenant, the blessings from God are given at the new birth. See the difference between Deuteronomy 28:1-14 and Ephesians 1:3. In other words, the blessings of Deuteronomy had to be earned, but the blessings of Ephesians 1:3 were given to us by grace. They only need to be received by faith. Obedience in the old covenant was to the law. Obedience in the new covenant is to the faith (Romans 1:5 and 16:26). In other words, obedience to believe. Believe the Word, believe the terms of the new covenant in Hebrews 8:8-12.

By now you are probably thinking what all this has to do with parenting. Well, in a sense, everything. I have stated previously that what we desire from our children is heart change, not just behavioral change. Obedience to the faith is what we desire for our children and what God desires from us. Obedience to believe His great love and that, as parents and children, He is for us and not against us, that with and by His grace we are before Him, washed sanctified and justified (1 Corinthians 6:11). Of course, this applies to our children as they receive Jesus as their Lord and Savior.

So again, let this guide your parenting. You want your children to leave home not just behaving right but believing right. This ties in to the ultimate goal of parenting in chapters three and four. We want them to believe the love. Believe that God is for them. Believe the gospel of the grace of God. To live life expecting the favor of God to be with them wherever they go. Live life expecting good to come to them because they have the advantage-the grace, the favor of God. This is the reason we develop a relationship with them and speak God's love to them daily.

Furthermore, I would like to add a few guidelines here on helping our children face and overcome temptations, tests, and trials. Much could be said in this area, but in keeping in line with the theme of this book let me delineate eight important things our children need to know to overcome.

I will not expound on them much, since that would be another book.

1. A revelation of the love of God- Love makes us more than conquerors-Rom.8:37

2. A revelation of grace-Romans 6:14

3. A knowledge of the complete forgiveness of their sins-2 John 2:12, Colossians 2:13

4. An understanding of their right standing with God and that when they sin, they are still the righteousness of God in Christ-2 Corinthians 5:21

5. Knowledge of the gates the devil will try to use to tempt them-Prov. 4:20-22 (ear gate, eye gate and mouth gate). In other words, they need to use wisdom in what they listen to, set before their eyes, and talk about. It is hard to resist temptation when they have been listening to the wrong music and watching the wrong shows and movies.

6. Knowledge of how to use the Name of Jesus, the blood of Jesus, and the Word to resist the devil and temptations.

7. How to pick godly friends. The wrong friends can tempt our children to go in the wrong direction. When children grow up feeling loved and secure, as they grow older, they will generally make the right choices in their friends.

8. Knowledge that all temptations start in our thoughts. They need to know they may not have total control over what thoughts come to them, but they do have total control over what thoughts they allow to stay in the minds.

Parents, this is all something that you can help your children with since by the grace and help of the Lord, you are amazing parents!

CHAPTER THIRTY - ONE

FINAL THOUGHTS/SOME FINAL REMINDERS

It is very important that we do not let positive behavior go unacknowledged. Hebrews 11:6 shows us that God wants us to believe that He is a rewarder. Of course, we do not do things just because there is a reward, but the fact remains God wants us to believe that He is a rewarder. Hence, we have to conclude that rewards are good. When two of your children are playing respectfully, acknowledge that. A child that is learning to do good without being told should be acknowledged and rewarded. Rewards are different than bribes, which many parents utilize when they are desperate to have some peace in the house. Be led by the Spirit of the Lord as to what rewards to give.

Believe God to grant you favor with your children. When they open up their hearts to us is when real influence starts. Most important is that they open their hearts to God, but if they can't open their hearts up to us, then opening up to God will be much harder. So, the keys are practicing grace with our children, and confessing that you have favor with them. What if you are convinced your children do not like you? Keep practicing grace and confessing favor with your children. I doubt they do not like you, maybe just some (many?) of the actions you have taken. Smile, parents.

Proverbs 4:7 states that wisdom is the principal thing. Pray for God's wisdom daily. Even when you miss it as parents, God will not withhold His wisdom. In all your getting, get understanding, Solomon added.

Have communion regularly with your children, parents. Lead them to the Lord as soon as they can understand the death and resurrection of our Savior. Of course, take them to church with you. Not going to church is not an option. Look for a church that teaches grace and the love of God.

Endeavor to have them grow up in one church unless God leads you to leave a church. Teach them that attending the church God has for them supersedes decisions such as where to go to work. In our society people move across the country for a better job without determining if God has released them from their present church. Christians need to first find the church God has for them and the job will follow. Along this area, when one of your children wants to stop attending church, the answer is "No." As long as they are living off our efforts, they have to go. Be courteous, but firm.

Our children need to be taught about the dangers of alcohol and drugs. Just because you do not drink or use drugs, do not assume you do not need to teach them the dangers of drugs and alcohol. Our children will listen to us when they are younger. As a parent, study on drugs and get to know the warning signs.

Teach them to be street smart and hear the Spirit when it comes to who they can trust. They need to be aware and know there are perpetrators out there. However, do not scare them into taking care of themselves.

Allow your children to make age appropriate choices. You determine the choices such as do they want to go home now (from the park, for example) or play ten more minutes. Of course, they will want to play ten more minutes. Ten minutes from now they will think they decided what time to go home, but you had already determined that in ten minutes you were going home anyway. Let them choose between the red shirt and the blue one if you have already determined that both are appropriate to wear.

Along these lines, wherever possible say "Yes." Too many "No's" can be discouraging. For example, a request to go play outside can be answered, with "yes, as soon as you finish your homework," rather than "No way, you have not finished your homework."

However, do not take this to mean that telling our kids" No" is not grace. Many parents, in fact, are afraid to say no to their children due to the fear of losing their love. The big "NO" has its place when what they are asking for is contrary to scripture. There are parents who allow their teens to drink at home rationalizing that at least they are not drinking behind their back. There is no way to excuse this.

In reference to parents who fear losing the love of their children, let me be clear here. Nothing in grace-based parenting should be construed that our goal is to become their friend. Absolutely not. Yes, we want a relationship with them, but the Lord will cause this to occur as we lean on His grace and leading of the Holy Spirit. We will not MAKE it happen. Trust God that when we say no to our children the Lord will be honored and work on the lives of our children. However, as they get older, they can start seeing us as their friend.

Get to know their friends. Go to their school events. Become a parent involved in their lives. Prepare yourselves for the big day that they will leave home (if they have not left yet). It bears repeating, accept God's forgiveness when you miss it.

Teach them the integrity of the Word of God and how to stand on the promises in the Bible. The best way to do this is when a challenge presents itself in their lives (such as a difficult class), teach them how to find a promise or promises in the Bible that relate to the challenge and how to stand on the scriptures. Speaking the promises and calling things that are not yet visible as if they were (Romans 4:17) is priceless. Faith speaks, as noted in 2 Corinthians 4:13.

Teach them how to pray by precept and practice. In other words, let them see you praying, but also teach them what a biblically correct prayer is. Buy them the books *Prayers That Avail Much for Children* and *Prayers That Avail Much for Teens*. However, do not forget to pray <u>with</u> them. Do not make prayer a law. Developing a relationship with Jesus is the essence of prayer, not how long we pray or that every prayer be exactly right.

Get them their own Bible and assign Bible passages for them to read and discuss with them. This is just a suggestion. Do what works. You do not always have to have a set time for devotions. Devotions may be in the car when you are picking them up from school as the opportunity arises. It bears restating not to make a law out of anything spiritual we are encouraging our children to do. Tithing is good and should be taught to our children, but not as a law. In the new covenant, there is no curse (Malachi 3:8-9), but we tithe as a response to our love for and trust in God. Related to this, teach budgeting and the need to save.

Returning to what I mentioned previously about our children living in a terror-filled world, teach them how to speak Psalm 91 over themselves. Furthermore, train them to speak the blood of Jesus over themselves and their school. Never let them leave home without you speaking the blood of Jesus over them and portions of Psalm 91.

Teach them how to set goals, and yet as they reach a goal encourage them to thank God and not their own efforts. They need to know that their goals were reached by the grace of God. If they go out for a sport, do not let them quit when the practices get long. In doing these things, you are preparing them for life. When you assign chores, go inspect them and if not properly done, have them redo them. This is definitely training them for when they start working part-time after school. All teens when they can legally work should do so.

Believe God to help you look upon them with favor, to see them as God sees them. And you, my friends, see yourself as God sees you. You are His beloved, the apple of His eye, His masterpiece (Ephesians 2:10 NLT), the very righteousness of God in Christ, AND an amazing parent! Thanks for taking time to read this book. I now speak God's grace over you and your children from Numbers 6:24-27 (NLT).

May the Lord bless you and protect you and your children. May He smile on you and be gracious to you and them. I speak His favor and peace over you and all your children. I speak great grace over you and them.

I call you an amazing parent and that your children as disciples taught by the Lord (Isaiah 54:13) are amazing children!

PROMISES TO PARENTS

Deuteronomy 28:4- "Blessed shall be the fruit of your body."

Psalm 112:1-2- "Blessed is the man who fears the Lord, … His descendants will be mighty on earth."

Psalm 127:3- "Behold, children are a heritage from the Lord, the fruit of the womb is His reward."

Psalm 128:3- "Your children (shall be) like olive plants all around your table."

Proverbs 13:1- "A Wise son heeds his father's instruction."

Proverbs 15:20- "A wise son makes a father glad."

Isaiah 54:13- "All your children shall be taught by the Lord, and great shall be the peace of your children."

Jeremiah 31:16-17 "Refrain your voice from weeping, and your eyes from tears; For your work shall be rewarded, says the Lord, and they (your children) shall come back from the land of the enemy. There is hope in your future, says the Lord, that your children shall come back to their own border."

Jeremiah 32:27- "Behold, I am the Lord, the God of all flesh. Is there anything too hard for me?"

Malachi 4:6- "And he will turn the hearts of the fathers to the children, And the hearts of the children to their fathers."

Acts 2:17- "And it shall come to pass in the last days, says God, That I will pour out of My Spirit on all flesh; Your sons and your daughters shall prophecy."

GRACE-FILLED WORDS

You are God's masterpiece.

You are God's very own child.

Wow! You did that?

What a joy you are in my life.

You bring so much joy to my life.

I am so glad you are my son/daughter.

I thank God for you.

You make me smile.

God loves you and I love you.

You are one of a kind.

You were so kind, or you were so thoughtful.

That is a great idea. How did you come up with that?

Thank you.

Good morning good afternoon or good evening. It is good to see you.

Good night.

You were missed.

God thinks you are great. So, do I.

SOME SHAMING STATEMENTS
TO AVOID

What is the matter with you?

When are you going to learn?

Can't you do anything right?

The trouble with you is that you never listen.

You are giving me a headache.

Shame on you, I taught you better.

You embarrassed me, or you disappointed me.

Look at this room-you live like a slob.

After all I have done for you.

Why can't you be like…?

How many times do I have to tell you?

Is that the way you want someone to treat you?

You forgot your jacket; how dumb can you get?

You will never change (or learn).

See these grey hairs?

The reason these are shaming statements is that they attack or put down the child and do not deal with their actions. Remember deal with the do and not the who. The list can go on and on. If you have used any of these statements with your children, do not condemn yourself, since you are an amazing parent!

ABOUT THE AUTHOR:

Samuel Martinez pastors Amazing Love Ministries, a church with English and Spanish services. FCF is part of the FCF fellowship of churches. He loves to teach on the goodness and the love of God. He was ordained in 1986 and has a master's degree in Marriage, Family and Child Counseling. Prior to beginning full-time ministry in 2001 he worked in the counseling field. He has taught parenting classes for over 25 years and has been married for over 48 years.

He can be reached by e-mail at Smartinez@cfaith. com or by regular mail at Amazing Love Ministries, 216 S Citrus P.O. Box 503 West Covina, Calif. 91791